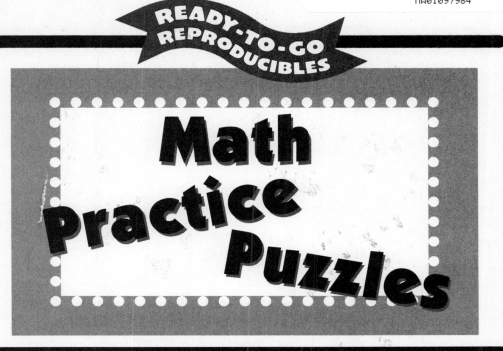

READY-TO-GO REPRODUCIBLES

Math Practice Puzzles

Multiplication and Division

by
Bob Olenych

SCHOLASTIC
PROFESSIONAL BOOKS

New York • Toronto • London • Auckland • Sydney
Mexico City • New Delhi • Hong Kong

DEDICATION
To Steve and Kristine with all my love.

Cover design by Kelli Thompson
Interior design by Melinda Belter
Interior illustrations by Steve Cox

ISBN 0-439-27167-3

Table of Contents

Introduction

Multiplication and Division Practice Can Be Super Fun!

Multiplication and division are two concepts I've always enjoyed teaching. Early in the school year, I emphasize these basic operations and encourage my students to learn their multiplication and division facts solidly. To help my students gain fluency and accuracy, I create skill-building practice puzzles and activities that they really enjoy—many of which you'll find in this book! These puzzles motivate my students to sharpen their multiplication and division skills and help them develop the strategies and confidence they need to tackle bigger mathematics challenges they'll encounter later in the year, including complex word problems and operations with decimals, fractions, and measurement.

What You'll Find in This Book

This book offers a collection of 40 multiplication and division activities for a broad range of skills and abilities. The book begins with activities involving multiplication, then progresses to division, and finally moves into mixed practice. The puzzles are arranged according to skill, from easy to difficult, beginning with basic facts and concluding with word problems. You can match the needs of your students and target a specific skill by checking the skill description, listed both in the Table of Contents and under the objective on each activity page.

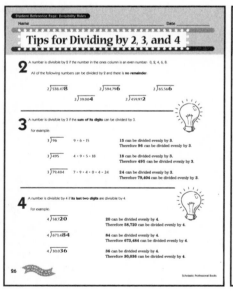
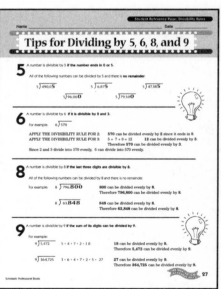

I've also included Tips for Dividing (pages 26–27), two quick-and-easy reference pages that my students have found especially helpful. These pages teach useful tips for tackling division problems with single-digit divisors. I usually assign No Remainders Please #1 (page 28) to review divisibility

rules for 2, 3, and 4, and follow with No Remainders Please #2 (page 29) to review divisibility rules for 5, 6, 8, and 9. Once my class has practiced these problems with their Tips for Dividing reference pages, I assess their ability to apply divisibility rules 2–9 with No Remainders Please #3 (page 30). This has turned out to be a very successful sequence of activities and my students' ability to accurately solve division problems has improved markedly.

How to Use This Book

Be sure to use these puzzles in a way that best suits the needs of your class. You may find it helpful to assign certain puzzles as practice work to follow a lesson, as review work, or as homework. You also may want to have students work on different puzzles depending on the skills each student needs to practice. The beauty of these activities is that almost all of them are self-correcting. Whether they are solving a riddle, breaking a code, or filling in a number puzzle, students are encouraged to check each problem so that they can finish the puzzle successfully.

Connections to the Math Standards

Most of the puzzles in this book target NCTM 2000 objectives listed under the Number and Operations standard. These objectives include understanding ways to represent numbers, determining meanings of operations and how they relate to one another, and computing with fluency and accuracy. This book is packed with exercises that require students to use the operations of multiplication and division in a variety of formats, including word problems and multiple step equations.

I'm confident that your students, like mine, will enjoy this collection of puzzles and reap the benefits of practicing these essential skills!

—*Bob Olenych*

Name _____ Date _____

Hot! Hot! Hot!

This multiplication grid contains 76 errors. Check all the answers carefully. When you find a mistake, correct it and shade in that box. When you have finished shading in the boxes with errors, the grid will reveal an answer to the following riddle.

What always stays hot even when you put it in the refrigerator?

X	8	5	3	2	7	6	4	0	9	2	5	8	1	7	4	3	9	1	2	6	0	3	7
2	18	7	5	8	14	12	8	2	16	1	7	16	3	12	6	5	18	2	4	12	0	6	14
6	42	30	18	21	42	36	24	6	54	12	35	48	7	42	24	15	54	6	12	36	0	18	42
7	63	30	20	12	49	42	28	7	36	12	30	56	8	81	27	20	63	7	14	40	7	20	48
1	9	5	3	2	7	6	4	1	9	2	5	8	2	7	4	3	9	1	2	7	0	3	8
5	35	25	8	7	30	35	20	5	45	10	25	40	6	35	21	18	40	6	10	35	5	14	36
8	64	40	11	16	56	48	32	0	72	16	40	64	8	56	36	24	72	8	16	42	0	27	56
4	32	20	7	6	27	24	16	0	36	8	20	32	4	28	12	10	63	4	8	25	0	12	25
9	72	45	26	18	63	54	36	0	81	18	45	72	9	63	63	27	81	9	18	54	0	27	63
3	24	15	6	5	20	15	12	0	27	6	15	24	3	21	14	6	28	4	6	18	0	9	21

READY-TO-GO REPRODUCIBLES

Name _____   Date _____

What a Mix-Up

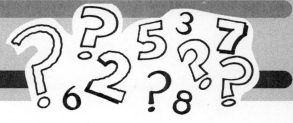

Here are four mixed-up multiplication charts. Find the missing factors and products to complete these charts correctly. Some of these charts may have more than one solution.

X	7	4	6	3
5				
2				
8			48	
9				

X	4	9	2	
3				
8		45		
7				42

Hint
In the charts with missing factors, you'll notice some of the products lined up in rows or columns. Use your knowledge of common factors to help you see how these products are related.

X				
	12		24	
		25		
	14			
9			27	

X				
	18			
				21
			32	
		45		

READY-TO-GO REPRODUCIBLES

Name _____ Date _____

Anxious Mother

Solve each of the problems below. Locate your answer in one of the boxes at the
bottom of the page. In the correct box, write the word that matches your answer.
Once you have filled in all the boxes, you will discover a question and an answer.

$(18 ÷ 6) \times (20 ÷ 5)$ = _____ = **SON** $(48 ÷ 8) \times (9 ÷ 3)$ = _____ = **HER**

$(24 ÷ 3) \times (16 ÷ 4)$ = _____ = **GHOST** $(21 ÷ 7) \times (40 ÷ 5)$ = _____ = **THE**

$(40 ÷ 8) \times (45 ÷ 5)$ = _____ = **SUCH** $(20 ÷ 4) \times (25 ÷ 5)$ = _____ = **BE**

$(49 ÷ 7) \times (56 ÷ 7)$ = _____ = **LITTLE** $(45 ÷ 9) \times (70 ÷ 10)$ = _____ = **WHY**

$(21 ÷ 3) \times (36 ÷ 6)$ = _____ = **TIME** $(24 ÷ 8) \times (36 ÷ 4)$ = _____ = **SEEMED**

$(54 ÷ 9) \times (35 ÷ 7)$ = _____ = **THE** $(14 ÷ 2) \times (20 ÷ 5)$ = _____ = **ALL**

$(81 ÷ 9) \times (64 ÷ 8)$ = _____ = **ALWAYS** $(63 ÷ 7) \times (54 ÷ 6)$ = _____ = **ABOUT**

$(30 ÷ 5) \times (72 ÷ 9)$ = _____ = **SPIRITS** $(70 ÷ 10) \times (6 ÷ 3)$ = _____ = **HE**

$(12 ÷ 6) \times (100 ÷ 10)$ = ____ = **WORRIED** $(42 ÷ 7) \times (18 ÷ 3)$ = _____ = **GREAT**

$(28 ÷ 4) \times (15 ÷ 5)$ = _____ = **TO** $(16 ÷ 2) \times (10 ÷ 2)$ = _____ = **MOTHER**

$(8 ÷ 4) \times (10 ÷ 5)$ = _____ = **WAS** $(56 ÷ 8) \times (9 ÷ 1)$ = _____ = **IN**

QUESTION:

35	4	30	40	32
20	81	18	56	12 ?

ANSWER:

14	72	27	21	25	63
45	36	48	28	24	42

READY·TO·GO
REPRODUCIBLES

Name _____ Date _____

Limerick Fun

Solve each of these division and multiplication problems. Record your answer in the space provided. Then locate your answer in the code below and write the letter from the problem in the matching code space. As you find identical answers, give those answers the same letter. One example has been done for you.

(24 ÷ 8) × 8 = __24__ = **G**   (48 ÷ 8) × 3 = _____ = **K**   (18 ÷ 3) × 7 = _____ = **U**   (27 ÷ 9) × 7 = _____ = **A**

(56 ÷ 7) × 2 = _____ = **I**   (35 ÷ 7) × 6 = _____ = **T**   (49 ÷ 7) × 8 = _____ = **F**   (54 ÷ 9) × 2 = _____ = **M**

(72 ÷ 8) × 3 = _____ = **W**   (10 ÷ 1) × 6 = _____ = **L**   (32 ÷ 8) × 9 = _____ = **D**   (50 ÷ 5) × 0 = _____ = **H**

(81 ÷ 9) × 5 = _____ = **Y**   (20 ÷ 5) × 1 = _____ = **N**   (21 ÷ 3) × 4 = _____ = **R**   (42 ÷ 6) × 7 = _____ = **C**

(15 ÷ 3) × 4 = _____ = **P**   (45 ÷ 5) × 9 = _____ = **E**   (40 ÷ 8) × 7 = _____ = **O**   (24 ÷ 6) × 8 = _____ = **S**

                                                                                    (16 ÷ 8) × 3 = _____ = **J**

__ __ __ __ __ / __ __ __ / __ / __ __ __ __ __ᴳ__ / __ __ __
30 0 81 28 81 27 21 32   21   45 35 42 4 24   12 21 4

/ __ __ __ __ / __ __ __ __ __
  56 28 35 12   60 81 81 36 32

__ __ __ / __ __ __ __ __ __ __ __ / __
27 0 35   32 27 21 60 60 35 27 81 36   21

/ __ __ __ __ __ __ / __ __ / __ __ __ __ __
  20 21 49 18 81 30   35 56   32 81 81 36 32

__ __ __ __ __ __ / __ __ __ __ / __ __ __ / __ __ __ __
27 16 30 0 16 4   6 42 32 30   35 4 81   0 35 42 28

__ __ __ / __ __ __ __ / __ __ __ / __ / __ __ __ __ __ __
0 16 32   4 35 32 81   27 21 32   21   56 60 35 27 81 28

__ __ __ / __ __ __ / __ __ __ __ / __ __ __ / __
21 4 36   0 16 32   0 81 21 36   27 21 32   21

/ __ __ __ __ / __ __ / __ __ __ __ __
  12 81 32 32   35 56   27 81 81 36 32

Name _____ Date _____

Equal Values

Solve the problems in both sets of boxes. Then match each answer in the top boxes to an equivalent answer in the bottom boxes. Discover the answer to the following question by writing each word from the top set of boxes in the boxes underneath with the matching answer. One example has been done for you.

Why did the comedian's wife file for divorce?

9 × 8 = **72** HER	32 × 3 = WHILE	17 × 6 = TRYING	49 × 4 = COMEDIAN'S	25 × 4 = DEATH
40 × 3 = THE	13 × 8 = HUSBAND	40 × 6 = THAT	22 × 8 = WIFE	36 × 5 = THE
26 × 6 = SAID	85 × 2 = TO	13 × 9 = FUNNY	57 × 3 = TIME	50 × 9 = WAS
62 × 6 = JOKE	47 × 4 = SOBBING	33 × 6 = HER	18 × 8 = ALL	35 × 8 = TO

20 × 9 = _____	28 × 7 = _____	44 × 4 = _____	52 × 3 = _____ ,	12 × 8 = _____
94 × 2 = _____ ,	30 × 8 = _____	24 × 3 = **72** her	39 × 3 = _____	26 × 4 = _____
75 × 6 = _____	34 × 3 = _____	34 × 5 = _____	93 × 4 = _____	66 × 3 = _____
70 × 4 = _____	20 × 5 = _____	24 × 6 = _____	24 × 5 = _____	19 × 9 = _____ !

10

Name _____ Date _____

G'Day

Solve the following problems and find your answers in the code boxes below.
Write the letter from each problem in the code box with the matching answer.
If the answer appears in more than one code box, fill in each one with the same letter.

What did the clockmaker say to all of his good friends?

Y $\begin{array}{r} 728 \\ \times\ \ 5 \\ \hline \end{array}$	N $\begin{array}{r} 309 \\ \times\ \ 9 \\ \hline \end{array}$	O $\begin{array}{r} 462 \\ \times\ \ 6 \\ \hline \end{array}$
I $\begin{array}{r} 581 \\ \times\ \ 8 \\ \hline \end{array}$	A $\begin{array}{r} 743 \\ \times\ \ 3 \\ \hline \end{array}$	R $\begin{array}{r} 980 \\ \times\ \ 2 \\ \hline \end{array}$
G $\begin{array}{r} 630 \\ \times\ \ 7 \\ \hline \end{array}$	H $\begin{array}{r} 997 \\ \times\ \ 4 \\ \hline \end{array}$	C $\begin{array}{r} 458 \\ \times\ \ 5 \\ \hline \end{array}$
D $\begin{array}{r} 297 \\ \times\ \ 6 \\ \hline \end{array}$	V $\begin{array}{r} 684 \\ \times\ \ 9 \\ \hline \end{array}$	S $\begin{array}{r} 893 \\ \times\ \ 8 \\ \hline \end{array}$
W $\begin{array}{r} 408 \\ \times\ \ 3 \\ \hline \end{array}$	M $\begin{array}{r} 796 \\ \times\ \ 7 \\ \hline \end{array}$	E $\begin{array}{r} 228 \\ \times\ \ 4 \\ \hline \end{array}$

912	6,156	912	1,960	3,640

5,572	2,772	1,960	2,781	4,648	2,781	4,410

1,224	912

1,960	4,648	7,144	912

2,229	2,781	1,782

2,290	3,988	4,648	5,572	912

!

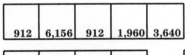

Name _____ Date _____

Cross Number Puzzle

Express each multiplication problem below in its numerical form. Then solve the problems and write your answers in the appropriate across or down positions.

ACROSS

1. Multiply five hundred eighty-six by five   _____

2. Multiply nine hundred eighty-eight by six   _____

3. Multiply seven hundred ninety-nine by six   _____

5. Multiply six hundred seventy-eight by three   _____

7. Multiply six hundred fifty-three by five   _____

9. Multiply seven hundred forty-seven by four   _____

10. Multiply eight hundred twenty-five by eight   _____

DOWN

1. Multiply three hundred seventy-three by eight   _____

2. Multiply seven hundred forty-six by seven   _____

4. Multiply six hundred nine by eight   _____

6. Multiply four hundred sixty by seven   _____

7. Multiply four hundred eighty-seven by eight   _____

8. Multiply nine hundred forty by six   _____

NUMERICAL FORM

READY-TO-GO REPRODUCIBLES

Name _____ Date _____

Cross Them Out

Solve all of the problems below. Locate and cross out each of the correct answers in the grid. (Answers run horizontally, left to right.) When you have finished, 35 boxes will remain. Write the remaining letters in order from left to right and top to bottom to reveal the answer to the following riddle. The first problem has been done for you.

Why did the service station mechanic always dress in disguise?

1. 5,096
    × 6
    30,576

2. 4,937
    × 8

3. 6,407
    × 7

4. 7,009
    × 3

5. 4,150
    × 5

6. 3,050
    × 9

7. 5,800
    × 4

8. 9,779
    × 7

9. 8,240
    × 6

A 2	C 3	R 2	E 0	T 0	H 4	E 9	A 7	L 0	W 4
A 5	Y 7	B 3	O 9	D 4	I 9	L 6	S 6	W 3	I 5
S 4	H 7	E 0	D 8	G 2	R 1	I 0	D 2	E 7	T 3
A 2	B 7	O 4	D 5	L 0	~~I 3~~	~~T 0~~	~~W 5~~	~~A 7~~	~~E 6~~
O 6	B 6	E 0	J 6	X 8	E 4	F 5	E 3	A 3	S 8
E 4	R 4	S 9	T 4	W 4	O 0	C 4	R 4	E 0	T 4
S 2	E 7	R 8	C 2	L 0	O 7	U 5	R 0	V 7	I 9
C 1	E 3	M 9	A 6	N 3	D 4	R 4	I 8	T 4	S 9

Scholastic Professional Books • Math Practice Puzzles: Multiplication and Division

Name _____ Date _____

Shapely Math #1

Study the shapes in problems 1–6. Each shape has only one match in the number grids at the right. Use the shapes to fill in the missing numbers in the equations. Solve each number sentence and find your answer in the Answer Box below.

81	32	65
47	90	68
78	55	24

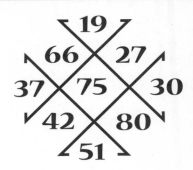

1. (65 x 75) − (☐ x ◁) = _____

2. (☐ x ◇) + (☐ x ◁) = _____

3. (☐ x ∨) + (☐ x ◇) = _____

4. (☐ x ▷) − (☐ x ◇) = _____

5. (☐ x △) + (☐ x ◇) = _____

6. (☐ x ◇) − (☐ x ◁) = _____

ANSWER BOX		
9,006	7,736	4,984
3,600	3,180	3,465
7,936	1,302	8,245

Hint
There are 3 answers in the Answer Box that you will not use.

READY-TO-GO REPRODUCIBLES

Name _____ Date _____

Politeness Please

Solve the 10 multiplication problems below. Write the answers in the across and down spaces in the cross-number puzzle. The number you record in the shaded box shows where the letter should go in the code at the bottom to solve this riddle.

ACROSS

| 1. | 773
x 56 | 4. | 319
x 48 | 6. | 687
x 82 | 7. | 470
x 84 | 8. | 916
x 72 |

DOWN

| 1. | 600
x 78 | 2. | 678
x 43 | 3. | 358
x 96 | 5. | 509
x 38 | 6. | 838
x 69 |

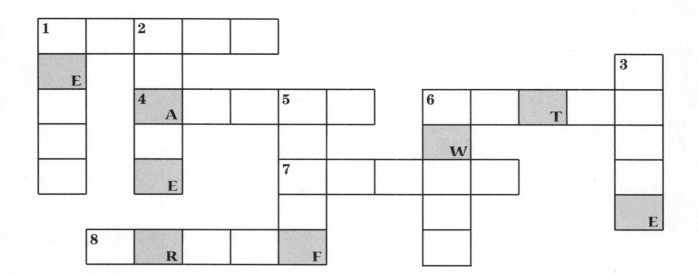

To prove he was a gentleman, what did the ram say to his girlfriend?

| 1 | 2 | 3 | 4 | 5 | | 6 | 7 | 8 | . |

Name _____ Date _____

Last Number-First Number

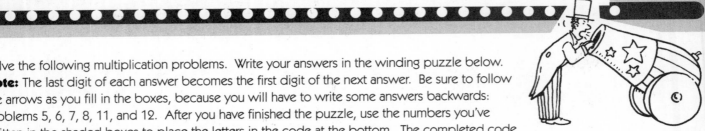

Solve the following multiplication problems. Write your answers in the winding puzzle below.
Note: The last digit of each answer becomes the first digit of the next answer. Be sure to follow
the arrows as you fill in the boxes, because you will have to write some answers backwards:
problems 5, 6, 7, 8, 11, and 12. After you have finished the puzzle, use the numbers you've
written in the shaded boxes to place the letters in the code at the bottom. The completed code
will answer this question:

What did the circus owner shout at his human cannonball?

1. 692 x 47	2. 706 x 62	3. 407 x 62	4. 905 x 53	5. 871 x 66	6. 781 x 86
7. 782 x 86	8. 518 x 47	9. 223 x 28	10. 589 x 71	11. 937 x 98	12. 808 x 75

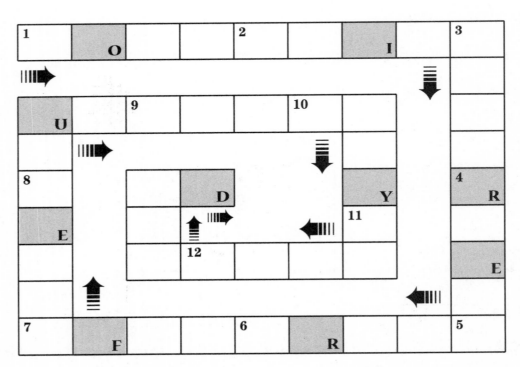

" ☐ ☐ ☐ ' ☐ ☐   ☐ ☐ ☐ ☐ ☐ !!!"
   1   2   3   4   5   6   7   8   9   0

Name _____ Date _____

Tic-Tac-Toe #1

Complete all of the multiplication problems. Look at the digit in the **ten thousands** column of each answer. If the digit is an even number, give that space an **X**, but if the digit is an odd number, give it an **O**. Any three **X**s or **O**s in a straight line wins.

445 x 659	308 x 750	913 x 404
862 x 600	823 x 328	447 x 709
924 x 156	703 x 905	121 x 989

READY-TO-GO REPRODUCIBLES

Name _____   Date _____

Number Search

Solve each of the division problems. Locate and circle the answers in the number search below. (Answers run horizontally and vertically.)

3,980 ÷ **5** = _____	1,470 ÷ **6** = _____	2,988 ÷ **4** = _____
7,578 ÷ **9** = _____	740 ÷ **2** = _____	1,708 ÷ **7** = _____
1,122 ÷ **3** = _____	4,968 ÷ **8** = _____	1,149 ÷ **3** = _____
3,563 ÷ **7** = _____	4,835 ÷ **5** = _____	4,614 ÷ **6** = _____
2,552 ÷ **4** = _____	3,429 ÷ **9** = _____	3,816 ÷ **8** = _____

6	3	8	**1**	**9**	7	4	7
3	5	8	4	6	7	**2**	**9**
7	**3**	**1**	4	7	7	5	6
7	7	**2**	**9**	**1**	3	7	4
6	0	**0**	6	3	8	4	**2**
9	8	4	**2**	3	3	2	**1**
5	2	7	**1**	8	**2**	4	5
8	7	5	0	**9**	0	**4**	2

Scholastic Professional Books • Math Practice Puzzles: Multiplication and Division

Name _____   Date _____

Break the Code

Why did the marathon runner go to see a veterinarian?

To break this code, solve each of the division problems. Then find your answers in the code boxes below.
Write the letter from each problem in the code box with the matching answer. If the answer appears in more than
one code box, fill in each one with the same letter.

847 ÷ 5 = **M**	545 ÷ 6 = **N**	706 ÷ 9 = **A**	469 ÷ 3 = **E**
964 ÷ 7 = **D**	627 ÷ 8 = **C**	943 ÷ 5 = **V**	908 ÷ 6 = **L**
473 ÷ 9 = **S**	389 ÷ 3 = **I**	763 ÷ 4 = **H**	347 ÷ 8 = **O**
761 ÷ 4 = **P**	687 ÷ 7 = **U**	477 ÷ 8 = **R**	937 ÷ 7 = **T**

| 190 r 3 | 156 r 1 |

| 78 r 3 | 43 r 3 | 169 r 2 | 190 r 1 | 151 r 2 | 78 r 4 | 129 r 2 | 90 r 5 | 156 r 1 | 137 r 5 |

| 133 r 6 | 190 r 3 | 78 r 4 | 133 r 6 |

| 190 r 3 | 129 r 2 | 52 r 5 |

| 78 r 3 | 78 r 4 | 151 r 2 | 188 r 3 | 156 r 1 | 52 r 5 |

| 190 r 3 | 98 r 1 | 59 r 5 | 133 r 6 | **!**

Name _____   Date _____

Crack the Code

Complete each of the division problems and find your answers in the code spaces.
Write the word from each problem in the matching answer space to solve the following riddle:

Did you hear about the male and female who got stuck in the revolving door?

$3,782 \div 5 =$	$6,784 \div 9 =$	$2,105 \div 7 =$	$2,578 \div 4 =$
DAY	**EACH**	**THIS**	**GOING**
$6,841 \div 3 =$	$4,579 \div 2 =$	$6,005 \div 5 =$	$7,063 \div 9 =$
STILL	**THEY**	**WITH**	**OTHER**
$5,937 \div 8 =$	$6,034 \div 4 =$	$4,938 \div 6 =$	$2,978 \div 3 =$
VERY	**AROUND**	**TO**	**ARE**

_____	_____	_____	_____
823	300 r 5	742 r 1	756 r 2

_____	_____	_____	_____
2,289 r 1	992 r 2	2,280 r 1	644 r 2

_____	_____	_____	_____ .
1,508 r 2	1,201	753 r 7	784 r 7

Name _____   Date _____

Water, Water Everywhere

What can go under the water and over the water and yet never touch the water?

Divide each of these problems carefully and locate your answers in the code below. Write the word from each problem in the matching answer space to solve the riddle.

1,308 ÷ 7 = **BRIDGE**	4,035 ÷ 9 = **HER**	6,170 ÷ 8 = **BUCKET**
4,030 ÷ 3 = **A**	5,007 ÷ 5 = **FULL**	6,304 ÷ 4 = **WOMAN**
9,078 ÷ 8 = **WATER**	3,804 ÷ 6 = **A**	5,406 ÷ 2 = **WITH**
7,630 ÷ 4 = **YOUNG**	4,260 ÷ 3 = **CROSSING**	3,720 ÷ 5 = **ON**
6,406 ÷ 2 = **OF**	3,900 ÷ 7 = **A**	5,004 ÷ 9 = **HEAD**

634	1,907 r 2	1,576	1,420	1,343 r 1
186 r 6	2,703	557 r 1	1,001 r 2	771 r 2
3,203	1,134 r 6	744	448 r 3	556

Name _____ Date _____

Tic-Tac-Toe #2

Complete all of the division problems. If your remainder is an even number, give that space an **X,** but if your remainder is an odd number, give it an **O.** Any three **X**s or **O**s in a straight line wins.

23) 13,480	47) 14,438	61) 30,507
35) 16,457	50) 29,154	67) 23,923
74) 18,651	19) 7,683	87) 19,665

Name _____ Date _____

Remainders

Solve the division problems below. Each answer has a remainder. Spell out the remainder in the cross-number puzzle. The clue above the problem tells you where the remainder should go. After completing the puzzle, write the letters from the shaded boxes in the matching code boxes below to reveal the solution to the following riddle. The first one has been done for you.

What can pierce your ears without leaving a hole?

1. **ACROSS**
   53,811 ÷ 67 = ___803___ r ___ten___

1. **DOWN**
   26,426 ÷ 47 = _____ r _____

2. **DOWN**
   73,726 ÷ 88 = _____ r _____

3. **ACROSS**
   19,211 ÷ 50 = _____ r _____

4. **ACROSS**
   29,630 ÷ 47 = _____ r _____

4. **DOWN**
   17,750 ÷ 36 = _____ r _____

5. **DOWN**
   49,502 ÷ 64 = _____ r _____

6. **ACROSS**
   30,104 ÷ 74 = _____ r _____

7. **DOWN**
   20,471 ÷ 54 = _____ r _____

8. **ACROSS**
   30,579 ÷ 39 = _____ r _____

9. **DOWN**
   17,384 ÷ 24 = _____ r _____

10. **ACROSS**
    14,934 ÷ 61 = _____ r _____

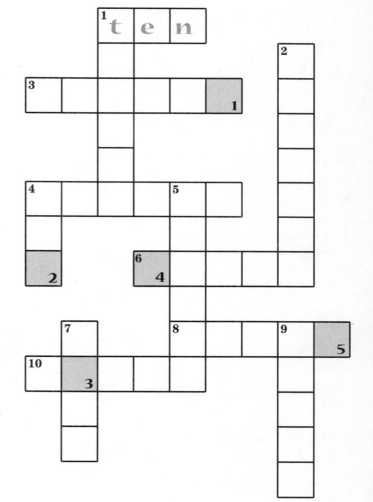

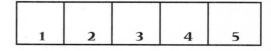

Scholastic Professional Books • Math Practice Puzzles: Multiplication and Division

Name _____ Date _____

Match It

Use division to solve the problems below. Then locate the correct answer in the column on the right. Use a ruler or straightedge to draw a line from the question to the answer (dot to dot). Your line will pass through a number and a letter. The number tells you where to write your letter in the code boxes to answer the question below.

After inventing lighter fluid, what happened to the inventor?

17,838 ÷ 24 = •   • 382 r 2

21,422 ÷ 32 = •   **1**   Ⓐ   • 281 r 13

42,719 ÷ 84 = •   **4**   Ⓞ   • 406 r 8

14,136 ÷ 37 = •   Ⓗ   • 150 r 22

18,703 ÷ 19 = •   Ⓕ   • 342 r 32

22,744 ÷ 56 = •   **6**   **2**   Ⓐ   • 743 r 6

36,475 ÷ 43 = •   **5**   **3**   **9**

                       7   Ⓛ   • 848 r 11

4,222 ÷ 28 = •   **8**   Ⓦ   • 384 r 4

                  Ⓜ   Ⓢ

20,210 ÷ 59 = •   **10**   Ⓤ   • 508 r 47

                            11

11,815 ÷ 42 = •   • 411 r 3

26,884 ÷ 70 = •   Ⓢ   Ⓔ   • 984 r 7

              12

25,485 ÷ 62 = •   • 669 r 14

1	2		3	4	5		6	7	8	9	10	11	12

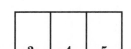

Name _____ Date _____

What Are There 76 Of?

The divisor in each of the following problems is 76. The multiples of 76, from 0 to 9, are listed below. Complete each of the problems carefully and locate your answer in the code box. Then fill in the matching letter to solve the riddle.

Multiples of 76
76 x 0 = 0
76 x 1 = 76
76 x 2 = 152
76 x 3 = 228
76 x 4 = 304
76 x 5 = 380
76 x 6 = 456
76 x 7 = 532
76 x 8 = 608
76 x 9 = 684

N
$76 \overline{) 5,978}$

M
$76 \overline{) 3,947}$

R
$76 \overline{) 2,776}$

O
$76 \overline{) 9,304}$

O
$76 \overline{) 6,037}$

E
$76 \overline{) 8,172}$

S
$76 \overline{) 2,137}$

T
$76 \overline{) 1,993}$

B
$76 \overline{) 3,676}$

26 r 17	36 r 40	122 r 32	51 r 71	48 r 28	79 r 33	78 r 50	107 r 40	28 r 9

READY-TO-GO REPRODUCIBLES

25

Name _____ Date _____

Tips for Dividing by 2, 3, and 4

2 A number is divisible by 2 if the number in the ones column is an even number: 0, 2, 4, 6, 8.

All of the following numbers can be divided by 2 and there is **no remainder**:

$$2\overline{)538,47\mathbf{8}} \qquad 2\overline{)594,79\mathbf{6}} \qquad 2\overline{)65,56\mathbf{6}}$$

$$2\overline{)39,00\mathbf{4}} \qquad 2\overline{)459,97\mathbf{2}}$$

3 A number is divisible by 3 if the **sum of its digits** can be divided by 3.

For example:

$$3\overline{)96} \qquad 9 + 6 = 15 \qquad$$ **15** can be divided evenly by **3**.
Therefore **96** can be divided evenly by **3**.

$$3\overline{)495} \qquad 4 + 9 + 5 = 18 \qquad$$ **18** can be divided evenly by **3**.
Therefore **495** can be divided evenly by **3**.

$$3\overline{)79,404} \qquad 7 + 9 + 4 + 0 + 4 = 24 \qquad$$ **24** can be divided evenly by **3**.
Therefore **79,404** can be divided evenly by **3**.

4 A number is divisible by 4 if **its last two digits** are divisible by 4.

For example:

$$4\overline{)58,7\mathbf{20}} \qquad$$ **20** can be divided evenly by **4**.
Therefore **58,720** can be divided evenly by **4**.

$$4\overline{)673,4\mathbf{84}} \qquad$$ **84** can be divided evenly by **4**.
Therefore **673,484** can be divided evenly by **4**.

$$4\overline{)30,0\mathbf{36}} \qquad$$ **36** can be divided evenly by **4**.
Therefore **30,036** can be divided evenly by **4**.

26

READY-TO-GO REPRODUCIBLES

Name _____ Date _____

Tips for Dividing by 5, 6, 8, and 9

5 A number is divisible by 5 **if the number ends in 0 or 5.**

All of the following numbers can be divided by 5 and there is **no remainder**:

$$5 \overline{)490,0\mathbf{5}} \qquad 5 \overline{)6,87\mathbf{5}} \qquad 5 \overline{)47,38\mathbf{5}}$$

$$5 \overline{)96,06\mathbf{0}} \qquad 5 \overline{)79,50\mathbf{0}}$$

---

6 A number is divisible by 6 **if it is divisible by 2 and 3.**

For example: $6 \overline{)570}$

APPLY THE DIVISIBILITY RULE FOR 2:   **570** can be divided evenly by **2** since it ends in **0**.
APPLY THE DIVISIBILITY RULE FOR 3: $5 + 7 + 0 = 12$ **12** can be divided evenly by **3**.
                                     Therefore **570** can be divided evenly by **3**.
Since 2 and 3 divide into 570 evenly, 6 can divide into 570 evenly.

---

8 A number is divisible by 8 **if the last three digits are divisible by 8.**

All of the following numbers can be divided by 8 and there is no remainder.

For example: $8 \overline{)796,\mathbf{800}}$ **800** can be divided evenly by **8**.
                                         Therefore **796,800** can be divided evenly by **8**.

$8 \overline{)63,\mathbf{848}}$ **848** can be divided evenly by **8**.
                                         Therefore **63,848** can be divided evenly by **8**.

---

9 A number is divisible by 9 **if the sum of its digits can be divided by 9.**

For example:

$9 \overline{)5,472}$ $5 + 4 + 7 + 2 = 18$ **18** can be divided evenly by **9**.
                                         Therefore **5,472** can be divided evenly by **9**.

$9 \overline{)364,725}$ $3 + 6 + 4 + 7 + 2 + 5 = 27$ **27** can be divided evenly by **9**.
                                         Therefore **364,725** can be divided evenly by **9**.

Name _____   Date _____

No Remainders Please #1

Apply the divisibility rules found on page 26 to the following problems. **Determine which of the problems can be divided with no remainder. Then solve only those problems.** Write the words from the problems you've solved in the matching answer spaces below to find the answer to the following riddle:

Which of these two travels faster, heat or cold?

YOU	HEAT	ANY	WITHOUT	TO
$79,608 \div 2$	$2 \overline{)\ 90,076}$	$6,943 \div 2$	$2 \overline{)\ 97,659}$	$2 \overline{)\ 36,740}$
CATCH	IT	FURTHER	CAN	BECAUSE
$3 \overline{)\ 73,041}$	$97,422 \div 3$	$3 \overline{)\ 7,775}$	$48,846 \div 3$	$94,563 \div 3$
HAS	COLD	SERIOUS	DISCUSSIONS	BE
$79,632 \div 4$	$4 \overline{)\ 34,588}$	$79,643 \div 4$	$4 \overline{)\ 59,461}$	$4 \overline{)\ 47,004}$

Answer

32,474	19,908	18,370	11,751	45,038

!

31,521	39,804	16,282	24,347	8,647

Name _____ Date _____

No Remainders Please #2

Apply the divisibility rules found on page 27 to the following problems. **Determine which of the problems can be divided with no remainder. Then solve only those problems.** Write the words from the problems you've solved in the matching answer spaces below to find the answer to the following riddle:

Why was the mother flea crying so loudly?

DOGS	CHILDREN	EAGER	SQUIRMY	HUNGRY	HER
$5 \overline{)96,300}$	$79,465 \div 5$	$5 \overline{)40,396}$	$34,678 \div 5$	$24,681 \div 5$	$6 \overline{)7,956}$
HAD	MOTHER	WAS	UPSET	REALLY	LITTLE
$15,822 \div 6$	$6 \overline{)40,075}$	$78,004 \div 6$	$6 \overline{)37,007}$	$23,513 \div 6$	$8 \overline{)65,488}$
TO	THE	ALL	ONLY	GONE	RAPIDLY
$8 \overline{)34,840}$	$8 \overline{)70,816}$	$9 \overline{)94,563}$	$57,842 \div 9$	$9 \overline{)18,189}$	$34,760 \div 9$
				SOBBING	FLEAS
				$44,437 \div 9$	$9 \overline{)34,782}$

Answer

_____ _____ _____ _____ _____
10,507   1,326   8,186   15,893   2,637

_____ _____ _____ _____ !
2,021   4,355   8,852   19,260

Name _____   Date _____

No Remainders Please #3

Apply the divisibility rules found on pages 26 and 27 to the following problems. **Determine which of the problems can be divided with no remainder. Then solve only those problems.** Write the words from the problems you've solved in the matching answer spaces below to find the answer to the following riddle.

What did the mother flea say to her children?

$98,361 \div 3 =$ _____ = **TAKE** $46,332 \div 4 =$ _____ = **WE**

$73,842 \div 6 =$ _____ = **OURSELVES** $27,847 \div 2 =$ _____ = **RUN**

$97,648 \div 8 =$ _____ = **DOG** $56,005 \div 5 =$ _____ = **OR**

$70,765 \div 4 =$ _____ = **CAT** $182,736 \div 9 =$ _____ = **A**

$36,549 \div 9 =$ _____ = **SHALL** $34,688 \div 2 =$ _____ = **WALK**

$34,050 \div 5 =$ _____ = **FURRY** $66,692 \div 3 =$ _____ = **JOG**

$39,408 \div 8 =$ _____ = **BY** $43,573 \div 6 =$ _____ = **SPRINT**

Answer

_____	_____	_____	_____	_____
4,061	11,583	17,344	4,926	12,307

_____	_____	_____	_____	_____ ?
11,201	32,787	20,304	6,810	12,206

READY-TO-GO REPRODUCIBLES

Name _____   Date _____

Shapely Math #2

Study the shapes in equations 1–6. Each shape has only one match in the number grids at the right. Use the shapes to fill in the missing numbers in the equations. Solve each number sentence and find your answer in the Answer Box below.

190	585	329
640	144	303
600	880	252

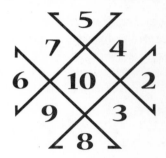

1. (190 ÷ 5) x (☐ ÷ ◇) = _____

2. (☐ ÷ ▷) x (☐ ÷ △) = _____

3. (☐ ÷ ▷) x (☐ ÷ ◇) = _____

4. (☐ ÷ ▷) x (☐ ÷ ◇) = _____

5. (☐ ÷ ◇) x (☐ ÷ ◁) = _____

6. (☐ ÷ ▽) x (☐ ÷ ◇) = _____

Hint
There are 3 answers in the Answer Box that you will not use.

ANSWER BOX		
3,600	4,212	3,760
2,599	7,482	8,360
2,470	5,080	2,424

READY-TO-GO REPRODUCIBLES

Name _____ Date _____

Links

Solve each problem, working from left to right. When you finish a problem, locate the answer in the box below, and write the letter above the answer to solve the riddle.

Take **93** → Multiply by **64** → Subtract **350** → Divide by **6** = _____ = **W**

Take **7,936** → Divide by **4** → Add **34** → Multiply by **7** = _____ = **E**

Take **950** → Subtract **266** → Multiply by **8** → Divide by **6** = _____ = **O**

Take **807** → Add **2,322** → Divide by **3** → Multiply by **8** = _____ = **L**

Take **375** → Divide by **5** → Multiply by **39** → Subtract **467** = _____ = **H**

Take **68** → Multiply by **49** → Divide by **4** → Add **1,257** = _____ = **L**

Take **4,394** → Add **3,342** → Divide by **8** → Subtract **72** = _____ = **S**

Take **3,940** → Subtract **978** → Add **588** → Divide by **8** = _____ = **T**

Take **71** → Add **2,934** → Divide by **5** → Multiply by **7** = _____ = **W**

Take **38** → Multiply by **88** → Divide by **4** → Add **427** = _____ = **A**

Of all the birds in the world, which one can be heard at every meal?

443 r 6	2,458	14,126

895	4,207	1,263	8,344	2,090	912	933 r 4

Scholastic Professional Books • Math Practice Puzzles: Multiplication and Division

READY-TO-GO REPRODUCIBLES

Name _____ Date _____

Follow the Arrows

Begin at the ☆. Solve the first multiplication problem and write your answer in the box directly below the problem. Follow the arrow to the next box and copy your answer from the first box. Solve the next problem, follow the arrow, and copy your new answer in the next open box. Continue to solve the problems, copying each answer into the next box indicated by the arrow. When you've finished the puzzle correctly, your final answer should be the exact number needed to solve the final problem. Go on to the second puzzle and follow the same steps you used to work your way through the first one!

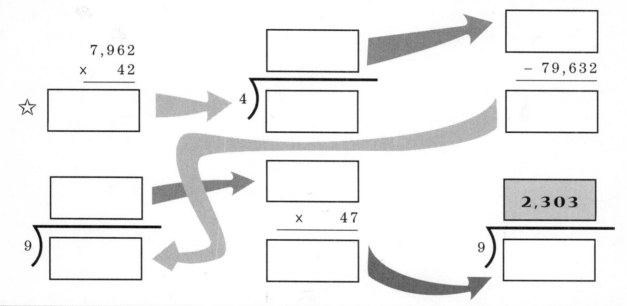

$$7{,}962 \times 42$$

$$4\overline{)}$$

$$- 79{,}632$$

$$9\overline{)}$$

$$\times 47$$

2,303

$$9\overline{)}$$

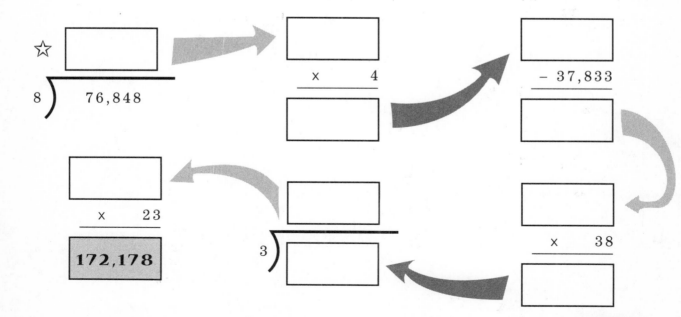

$$8\overline{)76{,}848}$$

$$\times 4$$

$$- 37{,}833$$

$$\times 38$$

$$3\overline{)}$$

$$\times 23$$

172,178

Name _____   Date _____

Super Code

Solve all of the problems that give you numbers to work with. Some of the answers you get will be used to solve the problems that have letter values. When you complete a problem, locate the answer in the code box below. Then write the the letter from that problem in that box. If the answer appears in more than one box, fill in each box with the same letter.

How do you get a squirrel to leave a tree?

P = 245×6 =   **R** = 38×42 =

N = $(255 + 340) - 92$ =   **I** = $U \times A$ =

K = $N \times A$ =   **E** = $1,593 \div 3$ =

C = $A + E + N$ =   **D** = $R - N$ =

U = $P - D$ =   **M** = $54,972 \div 9$ =

A = $7,486 - 7,394$ =   **T** = $4,430 \times 7$ =

L = $9,848 \div 8$ =   **B** = $478 + 639$ =

1,126	1,231	34,684	6,108	1,117

377	1,470

92

31,010	1,596	531	531

92	503	1,093

92	1,126	31,010

1,231	34,684	46,276	531

92

503	377	31,010

!

Name _____   Date _____

The Ultimate Multiplication Challenge

To solve this problem, you'll need to make many careful computations. After you've multiplied the top row of numbers by the 5, the sum of the first row of the answer will be 45. The sums for each of the other rows, as well as for the final product, are shown at the right of the problem.

The numbers that you write in the shaded boxes match the numbers in the code box below. Write each letter from a shaded box in the code box below with the identical number. The letters in the code box spell out the answer to this riddle:

What kind of special table has no legs?

$$3 , 6 \quad 0 \quad 5 , 8 \quad 2 \quad 7 , 4 \quad 9 \quad 1$$
$$x \quad 6 \quad 3 , 4 \quad 7 \quad 5$$

								B			= 45
		T									= 45
			I				**A**				= 45
					E						= 45
M											= 54
	L					**E**		**T**			= 90

1	2	3	4	5	6	7	8	9

Name _____ Date _____

The Supreme Division Challenge

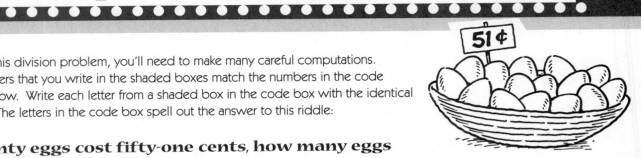

51¢

To solve this division problem, you'll need to make many careful computations. The numbers that you write in the shaded boxes match the numbers in the code boxes below. Write each letter from a shaded box in the code box with the identical number. The letters in the code box spell out the answer to this riddle:

If twenty eggs cost fifty-one cents, how many eggs can you buy for a cent and two quarters?

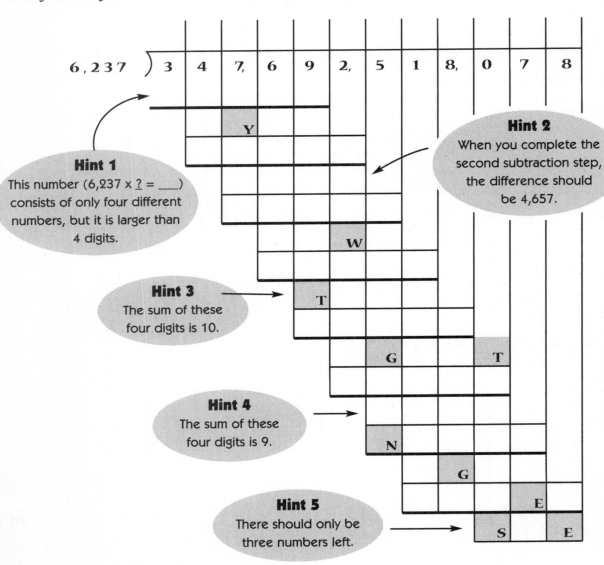

6,237) 3 4 7, 6 9 2, 5 1 8, 0 7 8

Hint 1
This number (6,237 x ? = ____) consists of only four different numbers, but it is larger than 4 digits.

Hint 2
When you complete the second subtraction step, the difference should be 4,657.

Hint 3
The sum of these four digits is 10.

Hint 4
The sum of these four digits is 9.

Hint 5
There should only be three numbers left.

| 0 | 1 | 2 | 3 | 4 | 5 |

| 6 | 7 | 8 | 9 |

READY-TO-GO REPRODUCIBLES

Name _____ Date _____

Lattice Multiplication

Lattice multiplication is a form of multiplication in which you use a grid like the one on the right. The example shows the problem 278 x 467. Here's how to solve it.

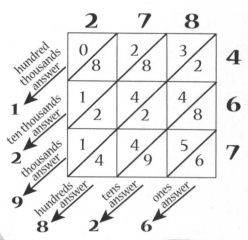

First, multiply a number in the horizontal position by a number in the vertical position (8 x 4 = 32). Notice how 32 is split into two parts by a diagonal line in the box that is placed at the intersection of the 8 column and the 4 row. Complete the rest of the horizontal and vertical multiplication to fill the rest of the grid.

Second, beginning with the bottom number in the box at the bottom right (6), add the numbers in each diagonal column. (Add only the numbers inside the grid.) Write the answer under each column. If your sum is greater than 9, use regrouping and add the carried number to the next column.

Third, find the answer to the original problem by reading the answer numbers outside the grid down and across. In this problem, the answer is 129,826.

Hint
In the tens column there are three numbers to add: 9 + 5 + 8 = 22. Since you can't write both digits in the tens place, you would write down the 2 ones and carry the 2 tens to add to the four numbers in the hundreds column.

Hint
In the ones column there's only one number, 6. Since 6 + 0 = 6, you would write a 6 in the ones place.

Now try these problems.

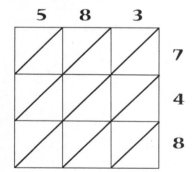

Make up two challenges by yourself.

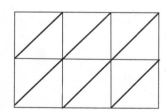

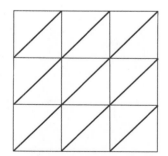

Hint
Check your challenge problems for accuracy using standard multiplication.

Name _____ Date _____

Let's Play Bingo

Solve the problems below and locate your answers in the bingo grid. Circle the answers you find in the grid. Any five answers in a line horizontally, vertically, or diagonally is a BINGO.

1. $(35 \div 5) - (63 \div 9) =$ _____ **2.** $(12 \times 10) - (12 \times 5) =$ _____ **3.** $(33 \div 3) \times (24 \div 4) =$ _____

4. $48 \div (2 \times 2 \times 2) =$ _____ **5.** $(21 \div 3) + (5 \times 9) =$ _____ **6.** $(50 \div 5) \times 10 =$ _____

7. $(24 + 12) \div 9 =$ _____ **8.** $(32 \div 4) + (42 \div 6) =$ _____ **9.** $72 \div (1 \times 3 \times 3) =$ _____

10. $(81 \div 9) \div (27 \div 9) =$ _____ **11.** $(60 \div 5) \div (2 \times 3) =$ _____ **12.** $(24 \div 6) \div (28 \div 7) =$ _____

13. $(8 \times 5) \div (32 \div 4) =$ _____ **14.** $49 \div (14 \div 2 \times 1) =$ _____ **15.** $(3 \times 12) + (36 \div 9) =$ _____

B I N G O

2	6	60	16	40
52	9	48	0	32
1	12	100	7	3
20	15	8	81	27
5	64	54	4	66

READY·TO·GO REPRODUCIBLES

Name _____ Date _____

Riddle Time

What did the angry baker say to her husband?

Complete the problems below to solve this riddle. Write the letter from each problem in the matching code box below. If the answer appears in more than one box, fill in each one with the same letter.

$(8 \times 8) + 4 = A$	A =	$(5 \times M) + 9 = 44$	M =
$(V \times 6) + 5 = 41$	V =	$(8 \times 4) + 8 = D$	D =
$(9 \times 8) + 3 = O$	O =	$(6 \times 7) + N = 45$	N =
$(7 \times Y) + 7 = 35$	Y =	$(5 \times 8) + 6 = P$	P =
$(4 \times 9) + 3 = Z$	Z =	$(L \times 3) + 7 = 34$	L =
$(8 \times 7) + I = 64$	I =	$(3 \times 7) + 7 = R$	R =
$(6 \times 9) + 9 = G$	G =	$(7 \times 7) + 8 = E$	E =

$(U \times 3) + 10 = 25$ U =

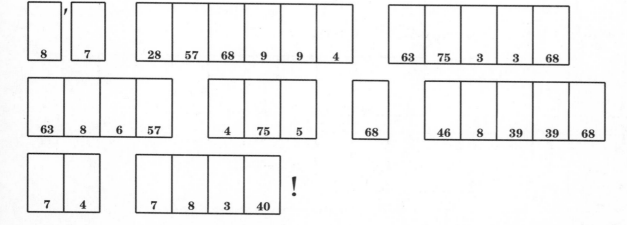

Name _____ Date _____

Order of Operations

Solve the following problems to solve this riddle. Write the letter from each problem in the matching code box below. If the answer appears in more than one box, fill in each one with the same letter.

C = $(45 - 5) \div (16 \div 2) \times (9 \div 3)$ = _____

M = $(25 \div 5) \times (36 \div 6) \div (100 \div 10)$ = _____

T = $(27 \div 9) \times (15 \div 5) \times (2 \times 1)$ = _____

U = $(5 + 2) \times (50 \div 10) \div (49 \div 7)$ = _____

A = $(63 \div 9) \times (16 \div 4) \div (10 \div 5)$ = _____

L = $(56 \div 7) \div (10 \div 5) \times (30 \div 6)$ = _____

O = $(3 \times 5) \div (45 \div 9) \times (21 \div 3)$ = _____

N = $(54 \div 6) \times (8 \div 2) \div (12 \div 2)$ = _____

Y = $(45 \div 9) \times (24 \div 3) \div (20 \div 5)$ = _____

R = $(48 \div 6) \div (4 \div 2) \times (16 \div 4)$ = _____

I = $(4 \times 9) \div (28 \div 7) \times (12 \div 4)$ = _____

E = $(15 - 3) \div (9 \div 3) \times (30 \div 10)$ = _____

What did the adding machine say to the cashier?

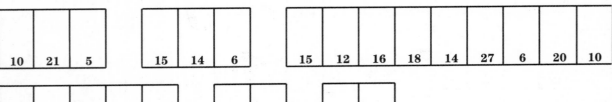

| 10 | 21 | 5 | | 15 | 14 | 6 | | 15 | 12 | 16 | 18 | 14 | 27 | 6 | 20 | 10 |

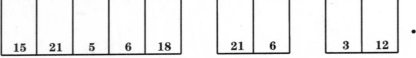

| 15 | 21 | 5 | 6 | 18 | | 21 | 6 | | 3 | 12 | •

Scholastic Professional Books • Math Practice Puzzles: Multiplication and Division

Name _____   Date _____

Code Breaker

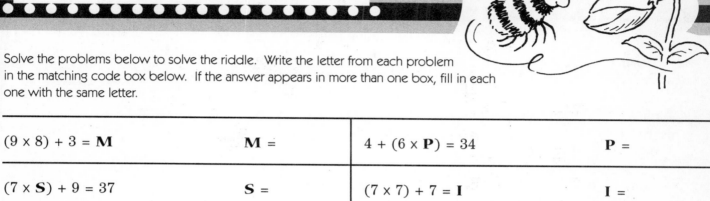

Solve the problems below to solve the riddle. Write the letter from each problem in the matching code box below. If the answer appears in more than one box, fill in each one with the same letter.

$(9 \times 8) + 3 = \mathbf{M}$	$\mathbf{M} =$	$4 + (6 \times \mathbf{P}) = 34$	$\mathbf{P} =$
$(7 \times \mathbf{S}) + 9 = 37$	$\mathbf{S} =$	$(7 \times 7) + 7 = \mathbf{I}$	$\mathbf{I} =$
$7 + (6 \times 8) = \mathbf{A}$	$\mathbf{A} =$	$(3 \times 3) + \mathbf{D} = 15$	$\mathbf{D} =$
$8 + (\mathbf{L} \times 4) = 40$	$\mathbf{L} =$	$(9 \times 9) + \mathbf{B} = 91$	$\mathbf{B} =$
$(4 \times 9) + 9 = \mathbf{N}$	$\mathbf{N} =$	$12 + (8 \times \mathbf{W}) = 12$	$\mathbf{W} =$
$(8 \times \mathbf{H}) + 5 = 29$	$\mathbf{H} =$	$8 + (3 \times 9) = \mathbf{Y}$	$\mathbf{Y} =$
$\mathbf{T} + (3 \times 6) = 25$	$\mathbf{T} =$	$(4 \times \mathbf{R}) + 8 = 16$	$\mathbf{R} =$
$8 + (7 \times \mathbf{O}) = 71$	$\mathbf{O} =$	$6 + (6 \times 9) = \mathbf{U}$	$\mathbf{U} =$
$3 + (2 \times 5) = \mathbf{E}$	$\mathbf{E} =$	$(5 \times 8) + \mathbf{G} = 52$	$\mathbf{G} =$

What did the polite bee say to the flower?

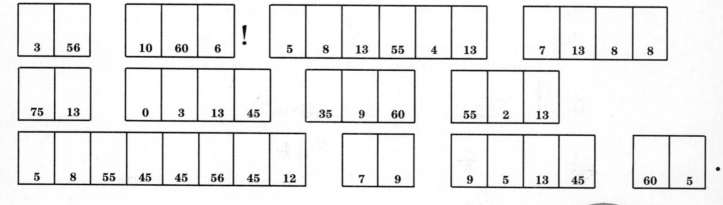

READY-TO-GO REPRODUCIBLES   41

Name _____ Date _____

Word Problems #1

Write your answer to each problem in the space provided. Locate your answer in the number search below. (Answers run horizontally and vertically.)

1. Maria is a voracious reader who reads two books each month. If the average length of two books is 514 pages, how many pages will she have read in one year's time? = _____

2. Section E of the baseball stadium has 25 rows with 40 seats in each row. How many fans can Section E hold? = _____

3. A traveling salesman covers a distance of 350 miles each day. He works from Monday to Friday only. How many miles will he travel in two weeks? = _____

4. A total of 34 students participated in a running club. After eight weeks of running, everyone had passed the 50-mile mark. What was the total distance covered by the entire group? = _____

5. On the busy Thanksgiving weekend, one of the customs officers at the U.S.-Canada border crossing interviewed 119 drivers each hour. How many travelers would have been interviewed in a 24-hour period? = _____

6. A bricklayer was hired to do the brick work on a warehouse wall that had no doors or windows. He calculated that he would need 298 bricks for the entire bottom row. If his calculations showed that he would need 46 rows, how many bricks would be used on this building project? = _____

4	3	7	4	3	6	1
7	5	5	7	2	4	3
9	6	1	6	8	0	7
0	0	7	3	5	0	0
0	8	0	0	6	7	8
1	0	0	0	7	0	9

READY-TO-GO REPRODUCIBLES

Name _____   Date _____

Word Problems #2

Write the answer to each problem in the space provided. Then write the word that is next to your answer in the matching code box below. Answer all the questions until you have decoded the following riddle:

Why does Betsy the Cow wear a bell?

1. The Year's Best Chewing Gum Awards are always attended by 4,200 bubble-blowing fans. If there are 25 seats in each row of the auditorium, how many rows of seats are needed to accommodate all of the fans?   = _____ = **HER**

2. Jamal and his classmates are participating in a reading club. The club will only run for two full weeks. Since Jamal's goal is to read 1,540 pages, how many pages will he need to read each day in order to achieve his goal?   = _____ = **WORK**

3. Orange juice producers have determined that it takes approximately 14 oranges to make a carton of orange juice. Since each tree yields about 5,530 oranges, how many cartons of juice would be made?   = _____ = **HORNS**

4. Eight friends had been collecting baseball, football, and hockey cards for three years. In total they amassed 11,552 cards. Because three of them were moving, they decided to divide the cards up evenly. What would each friend's share of cards be?   = _____ = **SIMPLY**

5. The Indianapolis 500 Speedway attracted 13,920 racecar fans. After the race, the spectators were leaving the parking lot at a rate of 58 cars per minute. How many minutes would it take for all of the cars to leave the parking lot?   = _____ = **DON'T**

6. A huge company picnic was attended by the employees and their families. The organizers purchased 1,587 hamburgers, assuming each person would eat three hamburgers. How many people were they hoping to have at the picnic?   = _____ = **BECAUSE**

1,444	529	168
395	240	110 .

Name _____ Date _____

Word Problems #3

Solve all of the problems below. Locate and cross out each of the correct answers in the grid. (Answers run horizontally or vertically.) When you have finished, 44 boxes will remain. Write the remaining letters in order from left to right and top to bottom to reveal the answer to the following riddle:

What is much heavier during the summer months than in the winter?

1. A Speedy Express driver travels 600 miles each day for six days. A driver for P.S. Post covers a distance of 650 miles each day in a five-day work week. How many miles does each driver travel in his or her work week? Who travels farther and by how much?

= _____
= _____
= _____

2. A group of 34 scouts were volunteering their time by planting seedlings. On the first day they planted 4,572 seedlings, but on the second day they planted 5,832. What was the average number of seedlings that each scout planted?

= _____

3. The driver of a large transport rig needs to replace all 28 of his truck tires. The tires are normally $483 per tire, but he received a discount of $12 per tire. What would it cost him to replace all of the tires on his rig?

= _____

4. A man was finishing a landscaping project, and he purchased eight mature trees at a cost of $980 per tree. The tree farm charged $120 to plant each tree. How much would the homeowner end up paying for the trees and the planting?

= _____

5. A woman was making some home improvements. She was replacing 12 smaller windows in her home at a cost of $169 per window. Three larger windows were $292 each. What did she spend on this project?

= _____

6. At one school, a successful fund-raising drive brought in $9,475. The school's goal was to purchase three computers at $2,435 each and a printer for $399. What would this purchase cost them? Would they have enough money for another computer?

= _____

1 T	4 H	3 E	6 C	1 R	3 U	1 S	8 T	8 E
5 O	2 B	9 E	0 A	4 T	3 N	2 S	5 T	8 K
1 A	3 N	8 T	7 U	7 A	0 B	4 L	7 T	0 U
4 R	5 A	8 F	4 F	3 I	7 C	9 F	0 L	0 E
0 O	7 W	5 H	7 E	3 J	7 A	8 D	3 G	4 I
7 N	0 G	3 R	4 T	2 D	6 O	3 T	5 S	3 H
5 E	0 S	0 O	3 U	5 R	7 N	4 N	0 G	9 Y
6 B	3 Y	6 O	0 U	0 R	8 E	3 A	5 C	8 H

___ ___ ___

___ ___ ___ ___ ___ ___ ___ ___

___ ___ ___ ___

___ ___ ___ ___

___ ___ ___ ___ ___

___ ___ ___ ___ ___

___ ___ ___ ___ ___ ___

___ ___ ___ ___ ___ ___

READY-TO-GO REPRODUCIBLES

Name _____ Date _____

Word Problems #4

Write the answer to each problem in the space provided. Then write the word that is next to your answer in the matching code box below. Answer all the questions until you have decoded the following riddle.

Why did the gang of thieves try to steal the baseball field?

1. If an estimated 15,000 cars crossed the Golden Gate Bridge within the first 15 minutes of a busy weekend, and the rate was maintained for a full hour, how many cars would have crossed the bridge? = _____   = **WORLD**

2. The traffic flow on the Golden Gate Bridge during rush hour was 33,000 cars for each 15-minute period for a full hour. How many cars crossed the bridge? = _____   = **THE**
How many more cars crossed the bridge during rush hour than during the busy weekend mentioned in question one above? = _____   = **BIGGEST**

3. The hourly traffic flow over the Golden Gate Bridge on four busy weekends was 102,836 cars; 123,709 cars; 355,200 cars; and 341,115 cars. What was the average number of cars to go over the bridge during the one-hour time span? = _____   = **THE**

4. A sightseeing boat had a very busy month of July. Each day the boat went out on three excursions with 50 people on board per trip. How many people did the sightseeing boat carry during the month of July if it went out every single day? = _____   = **IN**

5. Another sightseeing boat went out on Thursday, Friday, Saturday, and Sunday only. This boat made four trips per day with 35 people on board each time. How many people did they carry in one week? = _____   = **DIAMOND**

How many were carried over 20 days of sightseeing trips? = _____   = **IT**

6. Twenty-four thousand, six hundred eighty logs were sent down the river to the lumber mill. All of these logs were cut down by a crew of 20 loggers over a period of two months. What was the average number of logs cut by each lumberjack? = _____   = **ENTIRE**

If each log had a value of $79, how much would all of the logs be worth? = _____   = **HAD**

2,800	$1,949,720	230,715
72,000	560	4,650
132,000	1,234	60,000

ANSWER KEY

HOT! HOT! HOT! (p. 6)

x	6	5	3	2	7	4	0	9	1	5	8	1	7	4	3	9	2	6	0	3	7
2	16	10	6	4	14	12	8			0	18	4	10		2	14	8	6	18	2	4	12	0	6	14
6	48		30	18	42	36	24		0	54	12		30	6	42	24	18		6	12	36	0	18	42
7	56	35	21	14	49	42	28	0	63	14	35	56	7	49	28	21	63	7	14	42	0	21	49
1	8		5	3	2	7	6	4	0	9	2	5	1	8	9	1	2	6	0	3	7
5	40	15	10	35	30	0	45	10	25	35	5	20	15	45	5	30	0	15	35
8	64	40	16	56	48	32	0	72	16	40	64	8	56	32	72	8	16	48	0	24	56
4	32	24	16	0	36	8	20	32	4	28	16	12	36	4	24	28
9	72	18	63	54	36	0	81	18	45	72	63	9	81	9	18	54	0	27	63
8	24	15	9	6	21	18	12	0	27	6	15	24	3	21	6	18	0	9	21

WHAT A MIX-UP (p. 7)

x	7	4	6	3
5	35	20	30	15
2	14	8	12	6
8	56	32	48	24
9	63	36	54	27

x	4	9	2	6
3	12	27	6	18
8	32	72	16	48
5	20	45	10	30
7	28	63	14	42

x	2	5	4	3
6	12	30	24	18
5	10	25	20	15
7	14	35	28	21
9	18	45	36	27

x	6	9	8	3
3	18	27	24	9
7	42	63	56	21
4	24	36	32	12
5	30	45	40	15

ANXIOUS MOTHER (p. 8)

First column: 12, 32, 45, 56, 42, 30, 72, 48, 20, 21, 4

Second column: 18, 24, 25, 35, 27, 28, 81, 14, 36, 40, 63

Question: *Why was the mother ghost worried about her little son?*
Answer: *He always seemed to be in such great spirits all the time.*

LIMERICK FUN (p. 9)

G 24	K 18	U 42	A 21
I 16	T 30	F 56	M 12
W 27	L 60	D 36	H 0
Y 45	N 4	R 28	C 49
P 20	E 81	O 35	S 32
			J 6

*There was a young man from
    Leeds
Who swallowed a
    packet of seeds
Within just one hour
His nose was a flower
And his head was a
    mess of weeds.*

EQUAL VALUES (p. 10)

72	96	102	196	100
120	104	240	176	180
156	170	117	171	450
372	188	198	144	280

180	196	176	156	96
188	240	72	117	104
450	102	170	372	198
280	100	144	120	171

Why did the comedian's wife file for divorce?
The comedian's wife said, while sobbing, that her funny husband was trying to joke her to death all the time!

G'DAY (p. 11)

Y	3640	N	2781	O	2772
I	4648	A	2,229	R	1960
G	4410	H	3988	C	2290
D	1782	V	6156	S	7144
W	1224	M	5572	E	912

What did the clockmaker say to all of his good friends?
Every morning we rise and chime!

CROSS NUMBER PUZZLE (p. 12)

Across:
1. 2,930   2. 5,928   3. 4,794
5. 2,034   7. 3,265   9. 2,988
10. 6,600

Down:
1. 2,984   2. 5,222   4. 4,872
6. 3,220   7. 3,896   8. 5,640

CROSS THEM OUT (p. 13)

1. 30,576   2. 39,496   3. 44,849
4. 21,027   5. 20,750   6. 27,450
7. 23,200   8. 68,453   9. 49,440

Why did the service station mechanic always dress in disguise?
He always wished to be a secret service man.

SHAPELY MATH #1 (p.14)

1. (65 × 75) − (47 × 30) = 3,465
2. (32 × 42) + (68 × 27) = 3,180
3. (55 × 19) + (90 × 80) = 8,245
4. (78 × 37) − (24 × 66) = 1,302
5. (81 × 51) + (65 × 75) = 9,006
6. (90 × 66) − (78 × 30) = 3,600

POLITENESS PLEASE (p. 15)

Across:
1. 43,288   4. 15,312   6. 56,334
7. 39,480   8. 65,952

Down:
1. 46,800   2. 29,154   3. 34,368
5. 19,342   6. 57,822

To prove he was a gentleman, what did the ram say to his girlfriend?
After ewe.

LAST NUMBER— FIRST NUMBER (p. 16)

1. 32,524   2. 43,772   3. 25,234
4. 47,965   5. 57,486   6. 67,166
7. 67,252   8. 24,346   9. 6,244
10. 41,819   11. 91,826   12. 60,600

What did the circus owner shout at his human cannonball?
"You're fired!!!"

TIC-TAC-TOE (p. 17)

293,255 O	231,000 O	368,852 X
517,200 O	269,944 X	316,923 O
144,144 X	636,215 O	119,669 O

NUMBER SEARCH (p. 18)

1. 796   2. 245   3. 747
4. 842   5. 370   6. 244
7. 374   8. 621   9. 383
10. 509   11. 967   12. 769
13. 638   14. 381   15. 477

6	3	8	1	9	7	4	7
3	5	8	4	6	7	2	9
7	3	1	4	7	7	5	6
7	7	2	9	1	3	7	4
6	0	0	6	3	8	4	2
9	8	4	2	3	3	2	1
5	2	7	1	8	2	4	5
8	7	5	0	9	0	4	2

READY-TO-GO REPRODUCIBLES

Scholastic Professional Books • Math Practice Puzzles: Multiplication and Division

BREAK THE CODE (p. 19)

M: 169 r2	N: 90 r 5	A: 78 r 4	E: 156 r1
D: 137 r5	C: 78 r 3	V: 188 r 3	L: 151 r 2
S: 52 r 5	I: 129 r 2	H: 190 r3	O: 43 r 3
P: 190 r1	U: 98 r 1	R: 59 r 5	T: 133 r 6

Why did the marathon runner go to see a veterinarian?
He complained that his calves hurt!

CRACK THE CODE (p. 20)

756 r 2	753 r 7	300 r 5	644 r 2
2280 r 1	2289 r 1	1201	784 r 7
742 r 1	1508 r 2	823	992 r 2

Did you hear about the male and female who got stuck in the revolving door?
To this very day they are still going around with each other.

WATER, WATER EVERYWHERE (p. 21)

186 r 6	448 r 3	771 r 2
1343 r 1	1001 r 2	1576
1134 r 6	634	2703
1907 r 2	1420	744
3203	557 r 1	556

What can go under the water and over the water and yet never touch the water?
A young woman crossing a bridge with a full bucket of water on her head

TIC–TAC–TOE #2 (p. 22)

586 r 2	307 r 9	500 r 7
X	O	O
470 r 7	**583 r 4**	**357 r 4**
O	X	X
252 r 3	**404 r 7**	**226 r 3**
O	O	O

REMAINDERS (p. 23)

1. ACROSS 803 r *ten*
1. DOWN 562 r *twelve*
2. DOWN 837 r *seventy*
3. ACROSS 384 r *eleven*
4. ACROSS 630 r *twenty*
4. DOWN 493 r *two*
5. DOWN 773 r *thirty*
6. ACROSS 406 r *sixty*
7. DOWN 379 r *five*
8. ACROSS 784 r *three*
9. DOWN 724 r *eight*
10. ACROSS 244 r *fifty*

What can pierce your ears without leaving a hole?
Noise

MATCH IT (p. 24)

1. 743 r 6
2. 669 r 14
3. 508 r 47
4. 382 r 2
5. 984 r 7
6. 406 r 8
7. 848 r 11
8. 150 r 22
9. 342 r 32
10. 281 r 13
11. 384 r 4
12. 411 r 3

After inventing lighter fluid, what happened to the inventor?
He was flamous.

WHAT ARE THERE 76 OF? (p. 25)

N 78 r 50	M 51 r 71	R 36 r 40
O 122 r 32	O 79 r 33	E 107 r 40
S 28 r 9	T 26 r 17	B 48 r 28

Trombones

NO REMAINDERS PLEASE #1 (p. 28)

39,804	45,038	X	X	18,370
24,347	32,474	X	16,282	31,521
19,908	8,647	X	X	11,751

Which of these two travels faster, heat or cold?
It has to be heat because you can catch cold!

NO REMAINDERS PLEASE #2 (p. 29)

19,260	15,893	X	X	X	1,326
2,637	X	X	X	X	8,186
4,355	8,852	10,507	X	2,021	X
				X	X

Why was the mother flea crying so loudly?
All her little children had gone to the dogs!

NO REMAINDERS PLEASE #3 (p. 30)

1. 32,787
2. 12,307
3. 12,206
4. X
5. 4,061
6. 6,810
7. 4,926
8. 11,583
9. X
10. 11,201
11. 20,304
12. 17,344
13. X
14. X

What did the mother flea say to her children?
Shall we walk by ourselves or take a furry dog?

SHAPELY MATH #2 (p. 31)

1. (190 ÷ 5) × (585 ÷ 9) = 2,470
2. (329 ÷ 7) × (640 ÷ 8) = 3,760
3. (144 ÷ 6) × (303 ÷ 3) = 2,424
4. (600 ÷ 6) × (252 ÷ 7) = 3,600
5. (880 ÷ 10) × (190 ÷ 2) = 8,360
6. (585 ÷ 5) × (144 ÷ 4) = 4,212

LINKS (p. 32)

W = 933 r 4	L = 2,090
E = 14,126	S = 895
O = 912	T = 443 r 6
L = 8,344	W = 4,207
H = 2,458	A = 1,263

Of all the birds in the world, which one can be heard at every meal?
The swallow

FOLLOW THE ARROWS (p. 33)

☆ 334,404 ➠ 83,601 ➠ 3,969 ➠ 441 ➠ 20,727 ➠ 2,303

☆ 9,606 ➠ 38,424 ➠ 591 ➠ 22,458 ➠ 7,486 ➠ 172,178

SUPER CODE (p. 34)

P = 1,470	R = 1,596
N = 503	I = 34,684
K = 46,276	E = 531
C = 1,126	D = 1,093
U = 377	M = 6,108
A = 92	T = 31,010
L = 1,231	B = 1,117

How do you get a squirrel to leave a tree?
Climb up a tree and act like a nut!

THE ULTIMATE MULTIPLICATION CHALLENGE (p. 35)
Answer: 228,879,899,991,225

What kind of special table has no legs?
Timetable

THE SUPREME DIVISION CHALLENGE (p. 36)
Answer: 55,746,756

If twenty eggs cost fifty-one cents, how many eggs can you buy for a cent and two quarters?
Twenty eggs

LATTICE MULTIPLICATION (p. 37)

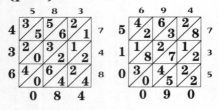

583 x 748 = 436,084
694 x 735 = 510,090
Answers will vary for student-created problems.

LET'S PLAY BINGO (p. 38)

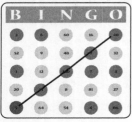

1. 0	2. 60	3. 66
4. 6	5. 52	6. 100
7. 4	8. 15	9. 8
10. 3	11. 2	12. 1
13. 5	14. 7	15. 40

RIDDLE TIME (p. 39)

A = 68	M = 7
V = 6	D = 40
O = 75	N = 3
Y = 4	P = 46
Z = 39	L = 9
I = 8	R = 28
G = 63	E = 57
	U = 5

What did the angry baker say to her husband?
I'm really gonna give you a pizza my mind!

ORDER OF OPERATIONS (p. 40)

C = 15
M = 3
T = 18
U = 5
A = 14
L = 20
O = 21
N = 6
Y = 10
R = 16
I = 27
E = 12

What did the adding machine say to the cashier?
You can certainly count on me.

CODE BREAKER (p. 41)

M = 75	P = 5
S = 4	I = 56
A = 55	D = 6
L = 8	B = 10
N = 45	W = 0
H = 3	Y = 35
T = 7	R = 2
O = 9	U = 60
E = 13	G = 12

What did the polite bee say to the flower?
Hi bud! Please tell me when you are planning to open up.

WORD PROBLEMS #1 (p. 42)
1. 6,168
2. 1,000
3. 3,500
4. 1,700
5. 2,856
6. 13,708

4	3	7	4	3	6	1
7	5	5	7	2	4	3
9	6	1	6	8	0	7
0	0	7	3	5	0	0
0	8	0	0	6	7	8
1	0	0	0	7	0	9

WORD PROBLEMS #2 (p. 43)
1. 168
2. 110
3. 395
4. 1,444
5. 240 minutes or 4 hours
6. 529

Why does Betsy the cow wear a bell?
Simply because her horns don't work.

WORD PROBLEMS #3 (p. 44)
1. 3,600–Speedy Express;
   3,250–P.S. Post;
   350–The Speedy Express driver travels farther.
2. 306
3. $13,188
4. $8,800
5. $2,904
6. $7,704; no

1 T	4 H	3 E	6 C			3 N	2 S	5 T		
5 O								7 T		
1 A	3 N	8 T						7 T		
4 R	5 A	8 F	4 F	3 I	7 C	9 F	0 L		4 I	
0 O	7 W	5 H	7 E		7 A	8 D			3 H	
7 N	0 G		4 T		6 O	3 T			9 Y	
5 E	0 S		3 U		7 N	4 N			8 H	
6 B					8 E	3 A	5 C		8 H	

What is much heavier during the summer months than in winter?
The constant traffic flow heading to the sunny beach

WORD PROBLEMS #4 (p. 45)
1. 60,000
2. 132,000; 72,000
3. 230,715
4. 4,650
5. 560; 2,800
6. 1,234; $1,949,720

Why did the gang of thieves try to steal the baseball field?
It had the biggest diamond in the entire world.